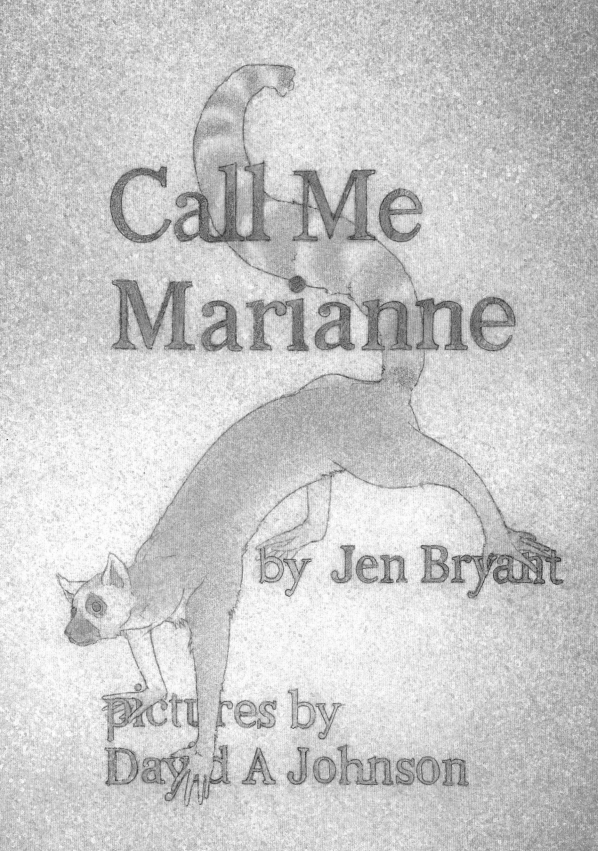

Call Me Marianne

by Jen Bryant

pictures by David A Johnson

Eerdmans Books for Young Readers

Grand Rapids, Michigan • Cambridge, U.K.

For my brother, Tom, who loves animals and understands how to really see
— J.B.

For August and Pat
— D.J.

Text © 2006 Jen Bryant
Illustrations © 2006 David Johnson
Published in 2006 by Eerdmans Books for Young Readers
An imprint of Wm. B. Eerdmans Publishing Company
255 Jefferson S.E., Grand Rapids, Michigan 49503
P.O. Box 163, Cambridge CB3 9PU U.K.
Manufactured in China
www.eerdmans.com/youngreaders

06 07 08 09 10 11   8 7 6 5 4 3 2 1

Library of Congress Cataloging-in-Publication Data

Bryant, Jennifer.
Call me Marianne / written by Jen Bryant ; illustrated by David Johnson.-- 1st ed.
p. cm.
Summary: A boy meets an older woman at the zoo, and together they observe
the animals while she tells him about the process of writing poetry.
ISBN 0-8028-5242-4 (alk. paper)
[1. Poetry--Fiction. 2. Zoo animals--Fiction. 3. Zoos--Fiction.
4. Moore, Marianne, 1887-1972--Fiction.] I. Johnson, David, 1951 Feb. 18- ill. II. Title.
PZ7.B8393Cal 2006
[E]--dc22
2004006805

The text type is set in Avenir.
The illustrations were created with ink and watercolors on paper.
Gayle Brown, Art Director
Matthew Van Zomeren, Graphic Designer

On Saturdays in Brooklyn, the city bus arrives
at half-past nine. I run to the corner
and hand the driver my dime.
"Getting off at the usual spot, Jonathan?" he asks.
I nod, and he punches my ticket.

On the bus, I study a page I clipped
from *The New York Times*:
"Exotic Lizards Have New Home at City Zoo."
A photo shows a lizard curled around a man's hand.

The woman across from me is dressed
all in black — black cape, black shoes, black skirt,
and a large black tri-cornered hat.
She's looking at the same picture
and making notes in a little book.

When she catches my stare, she smiles.
I smile back.
"City Zoo," cries the driver.
I get off behind the lady in black.

In the elephant pen, Daisy and Bernadette
are munching hay. Sometimes the keeper
lets me feed them peanuts through the fence.
But today I don't stay. I follow the snake-shaped signs
that point past the polar bears,
but when I turn the corner . . .

something tumbles in front of me.
It looks like a piece of black cloth
or a shingle that's blown off a roof.
It rolls along the sidewalk and bashes against a bush.
I run to pick it up, but the wind gets there first

and lifts it, whisking it ahead of me —
past the polar bears, past the flamingos,
the giraffes, the hippos . . .

past the kangaroos and koalas . . . until at last
it catches on a branch. I run, and this time
it waits for me, and I see
it's not a cloth or a shingle, but

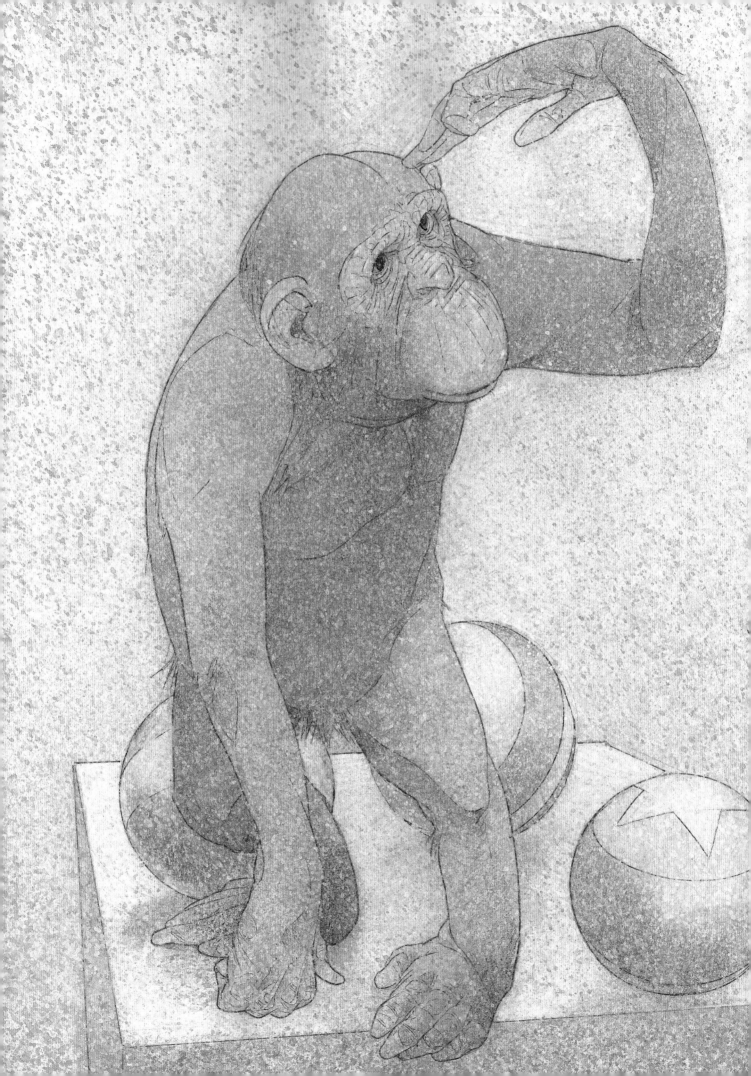

that lady's black tri-cornered hat.
I pick it up and brush it off. It's made of felt
and smells like roses. Inside, I find the initials *MM*.

A chimpanzee is watching me.
"I'd better give this back," I tell him.
"Where should I look first?" But he just
yawns and scratches his head.
Then I remember and run

. . . to the Reptile House.
"Excuse me," I ask. "Is this your hat?"
The lady jumps back like a scared cat.
For a moment, we stare at each other.
I'm not sure what to say.

Then she sees the hat and pats her bare head.
"Oh, my — I must have been busy scribbling.
I didn't even notice. Thank you, young man!"

She places the hat carefully on her head.
"My name's Miss Moore, but you can
 call me Marianne." She shakes my hand.
"And who might you be?"
"Jonathan," I answer, as politely as possible.

"Well, Jonathan," says Marianne, pulling out her clipping.
"I see that you and I think alike. Shall we go inside?"

The Reptile House is dark, but there are lights
in the tanks where lizards of all shapes and sizes
are scooting along logs or curving around branches.
Some are brown, but most are bright green,
the color of spinach or seaweed.

A few are resting on rocks, tilting their
crested heads this way and that, blinking
like patient cats. The big ones carry the small ones
piggyback. They seem happy and do not hurry.

We stand together very quietly . . . watching.
Marianne taps me on the shoulder and points
to the lizard that looks like the photograph.
He seems to be watching me, so I watch him.
I stand very still. He blinks. I blink. He doesn't move,
but then he sticks out his tongue. I stick out my tongue.

Marianne smiles. She opens her little book
and begins to scribble again. She's a curious lady —
I like her right away.

"Are you a scientist?" I ask. The question tumbles
from my mouth as quickly as the hat tumbled
across my path.

Marianne stops writing and looks up.
"No, I'm not a scientist — I'm a poet."

"Oh," I reply. I've never met a poet before.
"What, exactly, does a poet do?" I ask her.

She starts to answer, but more people come in
and it gets loud and crowded . . .

"Excuse me, please."

"Can you step aside?"

"Ouch, my foot!"

"Mommy, I can't see!"

"Wait your turn, dear."

"Let's come back later," I say.

We follow signs to Big Cat Country.
On the way, we stop to watch an antelope cleaning
her new calf . . .

and some monkeys leaping from loops of rope
to a trampoline . . .

and a mother bear teaching her cubs how to climb . . .

and the peacocks strutting and scolding,
unfolding their blue-green plumes like giant fans.

Marianne makes lots of notes.
She lets me watch, and when she's finished
she lets me look through her little book.

"Jonathan," she says at last. "Your question about
   poets is not a simple one. For me, being a poet begins

   with watching. I watch animals. I watch people.
   I read books and look at photographs. I notice
   details — little things that other people miss.

   Then I write them all down, I shuffle them around,
   like pieces of a puzzle, and I read them over
   and over out loud. And if I'm patient, very patient —

   and if I work, line by line, to get the words
   and the sounds just right, and the rhythm just right,
   then I make a good poem."

"Does it take a long time . . . to make a poem, I mean?"

   She points to a page.
"This one took me nearly a year!"

   I look at all the stops and starts — the crossed-out
   words, the circles and arrows, the commas and
   exclamations, the sketches and notes. At the bottom,
   the words line up in rows like obedient soldiers.

   She flips a few more pages.
"But this one took me only a few hours.
   Every poem is different — just like those lizards."

She pulls out a second book.
"This is for you — for returning my hat."
I open it. The black lines stretch across the page
like an empty cage, waiting for words.
"You could write poetry," Marianne whispers.

In Big Cat Country, Raja, the Indian tiger,
is napping, but a loud beep from the street
wakes him up. The driver waves.

"Let's meet here again," I say. "I'll look for your hat."
Marianne laughs and closes her book.
"Okay, but today *you* must write about the tiger!"

I wave until the car and Marianne's big black hat
are out of sight.

I rest on a bench in Big Cat Country.
Raja curls his paws around a piece of meat and purrs like a kitten.

For me, being a poet begins with watching . . . Marianne had said.

I take out the notebook and open it
to the first blank page.

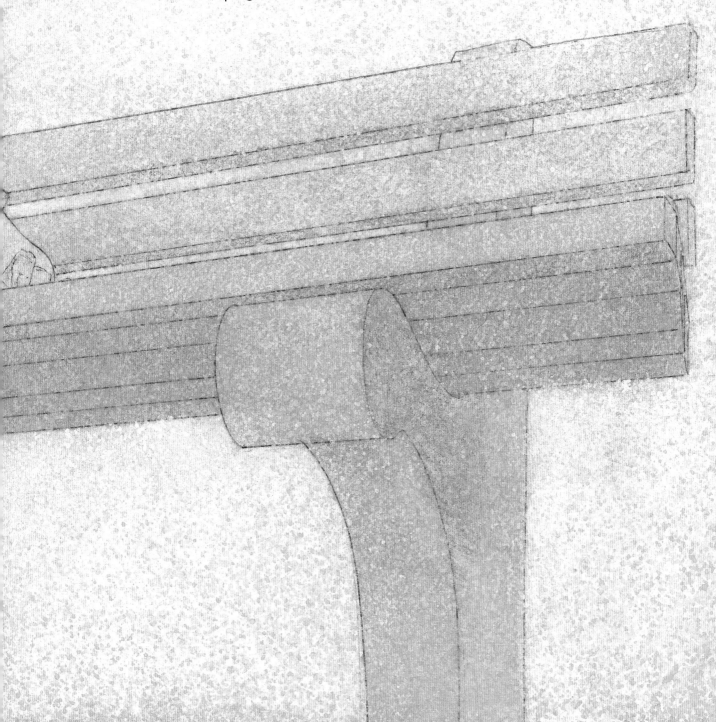

About Marianne Moore

Marianne Moore was born in Kirkwood, Missouri, in 1887, but she spent most of her growing-up years in Pennsylvania. When she was thirty years old, she moved to New York City, where she remained until her death in 1972.

As a student at Bryn Mawr College, Moore studied biology. She developed a lifelong interest in the natural world, in particular the appearance and behavior of animals. When she began writing poems, she often used animals metaphorically to explore the mysteries of human conduct, especially her own. "The Fish," "The Jeroba," "The Plumet Basilisk," "The Buffalo," "The Frigate Pelican," and "The Wood Weasel" are among her best-loved verses. Whether a species was spiny or slimy, feathered or furry, she found it unique, entertaining, and virtuous.

In New York, Moore often attended zoology lectures at the New York Public Library and at the Museum of Natural History, where she gathered details about the habits of various mammals, birds, and reptiles. A frequent visitor to the zoo, she was featured in a *Life* magazine article entitled "*Life* Goes on a Zoo Tour with a Famous Poet."

Like most writers, Moore guarded her privacy and solitude. But as her poetry became more popular, she became a reluctant public figure. Dressed in her trademark black cape (fastened under her chin with a silver dollar) and her famous tri-cornered hat, Moore appeared at museums, universities, formal dinners, and sports events. She loved baseball and was a great fan of the Brooklyn Dodgers.

This story is a fictional account of what might have happened on any Saturday in Brooklyn during the 1940s. In writing it, I made every attempt to remain true to what I believe Marianne Moore might have said and how she might have responded to a curious young person.

— J.B.